Cardinal McCarrick High School
310 Augusta St.
South Amboy, NJ 08879

# TOP TEN COUNTRIES OF RECENT IMMIGRANTS

# CUBA

## A MyReportLinks.com Book

### Lisa Harkrader

**MyReportLinks.com Books**
an imprint of
**Enslow Publishers, Inc.**
Box 398, 40 Industrial Road
Berkeley Heights, NJ 07922
USA

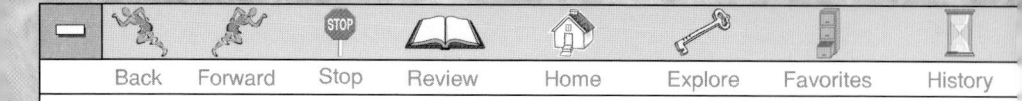

MyReportLinks.com Books, an imprint of Enslow Publishers, Inc. MyReportLinks® is a registered trademark of Enslow Publishers, Inc.

Copyright © 2004 by Enslow Publishers, Inc.

All rights reserved.

No part of this book may be reproduced by any means without the written permission of the publisher.

**Library of Congress Cataloging-in-Publication Data**

Harkrader, Lisa.
  Cuba / Lisa Harkrader.
      v. cm. — (Top ten countries of recent immigrants)
  Includes bibliographical references and index.
  Contents: Cuba, a land of beauty and struggle — Land and climate — Culture — Economy — History.
  ISBN 0-7660-5178-1
  1. Cuba—Juvenile literature. [1. Cuba.] I. Title. II. Series.
  F1758.5.H37 2004
  972.91—dc22
                                         2003012111

Printed in the United States of America

10 9 8 7 6 5 4 3 2 1

**To Our Readers:**
Through the purchase of this book, you and your library gain access to the Report Links that specifically back up this book.
The Publisher will provide access to the Report Links that back up this book and will keep these Report Links up to date on **www.myreportlinks.com** for three years from the book's first publication date.
We have done our best to make sure all Internet addresses in this book were active and appropriate when we went to press. However, the author and the Publisher have no control over, and assume no liability for, the material available on those Internet sites or on other Web sites they may link to.
The usage of the MyReportLinks.com Books Web site is subject to the terms and conditions stated on the Usage Policy Statement on **www.myreportlinks.com**.
A password may be required to access the Report Links that back up this book. The password is found on the bottom of page 4 of this book.
Any comments or suggestions can be sent by e-mail to comments@myreportlinks.com or to the address on the back cover.

**Photo Credits:** © Corel Corporation, pp. 1, 9 (flags), 11; AP/Wide World Photos, pp. 13, 29; Artville, p. 3; Enslow Publishers, Inc., p. 16 (map); Joseph W. Dougherty, p. 26; Library of Congress, pp. 37, 44; MyReportLinks.com Books, p. 4, back cover; NOAA, pp. 18, 30, 33; PBS, p. 24; Painet Stock Photos, p. 1; The Cuban Heritage Collection, The University of Miami, pp. 14, 35, 39, 43; USDA Photo by Peter Manzelli, pp. 22, 27.

**Cover Photos:** © Corel Corporation (flags); all other images, Painet Stock Photos.

# Contents

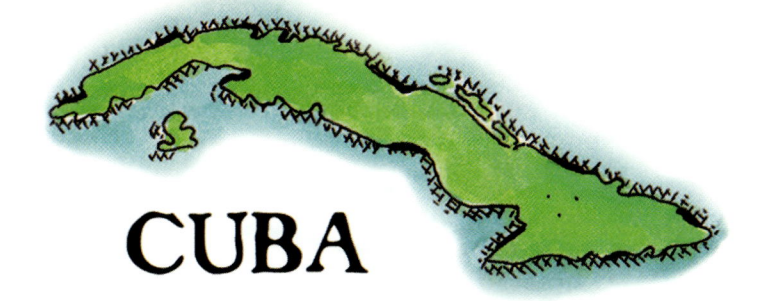

## CUBA

**Report Links** . . . . . . . . . . . . . . . . . . . . . . . **4**

**Cuba Facts** . . . . . . . . . . . . . . . . . . . . . . . . **9**

**1  Cuba: A Land of
Beauty and Struggle** . . . . . . . . . . . . . . . . **10**

**2  Land and Climate** . . . . . . . . . . . . . . . . . . **16**

**3  Culture** . . . . . . . . . . . . . . . . . . . . . . . . . **21**

**4  Economy** . . . . . . . . . . . . . . . . . . . . . . . **27**

**5  History** . . . . . . . . . . . . . . . . . . . . . . . . . **32**

**6  Cuban Americans** . . . . . . . . . . . . . . . . . . **41**

**Chapter Notes** . . . . . . . . . . . . . . . . . . . . **46**

**Further Reading** . . . . . . . . . . . . . . . . . . . **47**

**Index** . . . . . . . . . . . . . . . . . . . . . . . . . . **48**

Back | Forward | Stop | Review | Home | Explore | Favorites | History

**About MyReportLinks.com Books**

# MyReportLinks.com Books
## Great Books, Great Links, Great for Research!

The Report Links listed on the following four pages can save you hours of research time by **instantly** bringing you to the best Web sites relating to your report topic.

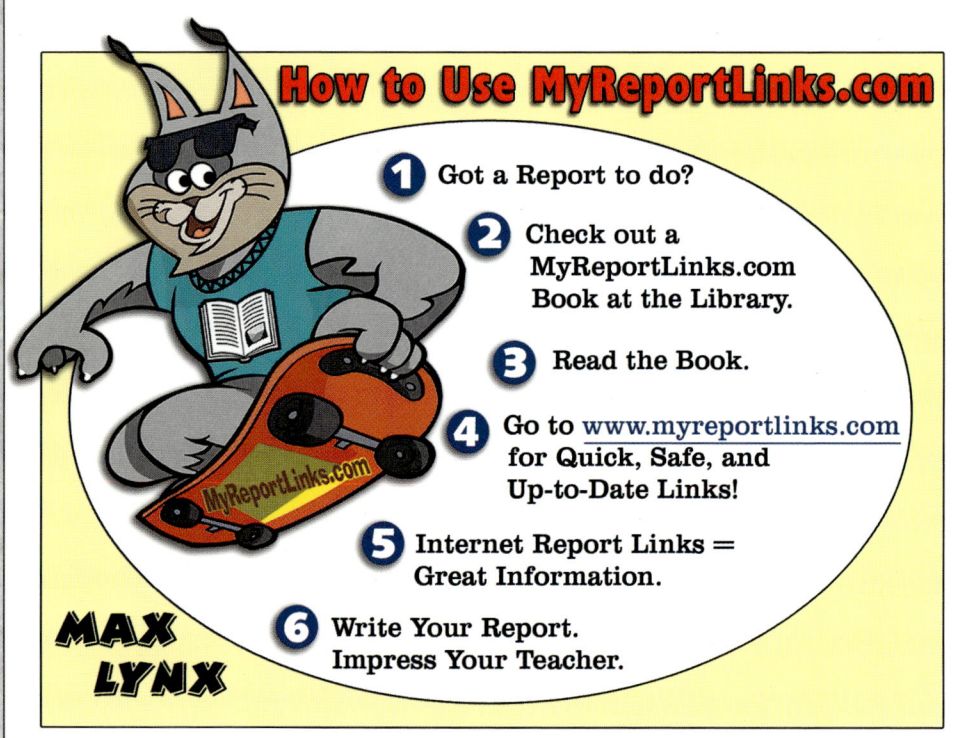

### How to Use MyReportLinks.com

1. Got a Report to do?
2. Check out a MyReportLinks.com Book at the Library.
3. Read the Book.
4. Go to www.myreportlinks.com for Quick, Safe, and Up-to-Date Links!
5. Internet Report Links = Great Information.
6. Write Your Report. Impress Your Teacher.

**MAX LYNX**

The pre-evaluated Web sites are your links to source documents, photographs, illustrations, and maps. They also provide links to dozens—even hundreds—of Web sites about your report subject.

MyReportLinks.com Books and the MyReportLinks.com Web site save you time and make report writing easier than ever!

Please see "To Our Readers" on the copyright page for important information about this book, the MyReportLinks.com Web site, and the Report Links that back up this book. Please enter **ICU8986** if asked for a password.

MyReportLinks.com Books

Tools   Search   Notes   Discuss                                              Go!

**Report Links**

➤ The Internet sites described below can be accessed at
http://www.myreportlinks.com

*Editor's choice

▶ **The World Fact Book 2002: Cuba**
The World Fact Book Web site provides a comprehensive overview of Cuba's people, geography, government, economy, and more.

*Editor's choice

▶ **Infoplease.com: Cuba**
Infoplease.com provides essential facts about Cuba, with information about Cuba's history, geography, and government.

*Editor's choice

▶ **Fidel Castro**
At this CNN Web site you will find a profile of Fidel Castro, including facts about his early life, education, family, and presidency.

*Editor's choice

▶ **Saving Elián**
*Frontline* explores the debate over the fate of Elián González, a young Cuban exile rescued from the waters off Florida, who was involved in a custody battle that affected Cuban-American relations.

*Editor's choice

▶ **Cuba and the United States**
PBS's Online NewsHour Web site explores the history of the relationship between the United States and Cuba and presents recent developments.

*Editor's choice

▶ **Stealing Home: The Case of Contemporary Cuban Baseball**
PBS's *Stealing Home: The Case of Contemporary Cuban Baseball* explores the history of baseball in Cuba and profiles Cuban baseball players who have defected to the United States.

Any comments? Contact us: comments@myreportlinks.com

| Back | Forward | Stop | Review | Home | Explore | Favorites | History |

## Report Links

The Internet sites described below can be accessed at
http://www.myreportlinks.com

### ▶Arnaz, Desi
At this Web site you will find a brief profile of entertainer Desi Arnaz. Born in Cuba in 1917, Desi Arnaz came to the United States and found success as a bandleader and as the costar of *I Love Lucy*.

### ▶Behind the Curtain: Cuba
This site from the *Washington Post* offers photographs of Cuba, providing a look at the country, its people, and its culture.

### ▶Buena Vista Social Club
This PBS site traces the making of a documentary about the Cuban traditional music ensemble the Buena Vista Social Club. The site also includes a time line of Cuba's musical history.

### ▶Castro Speech Database
At this Web site you can browse through a vast collection of speeches by and interviews with Fidel Castro from 1959 to 1998.

### ▶Cold War I: Bay of Pigs
At this Web site you will learn about the Bay of Pigs invasion in which Cuban exiles were trained by the Central Intelligence Agency of the United States to overthrow Fidel Castro's government.

### ▶Crucible of Empire: The Spanish-American War
PBS's *Crucible of Empire: The Spanish-American War* explores the war through an interactive time line. Here you will learn about the Ten Years' War, the Cuban War for Independence, the USS *Maine*, and much more.

### ▶Cuba
At the Lonely Planet Web site you can explore Cuba through a slide show, maps, and an overview of facts and history about Cuba.

### ▶Cuba
At this PBS Web site you will find a time line of Cuban history from 1910 to 2003.

Any comments? Contact us: **comments@myreportlinks.com**

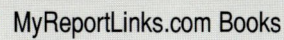

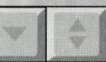

MyReportLinks.com Books

Tools    Search    Notes    Discuss                                      Go!

**Report Links**

The Internet sites described below can be accessed at
http://www.myreportlinks.com

▶**Cuba: A History of Religion and Intervention**
This ABC News Web site provides articles about Cuba's connection to Roman Catholicism, from its early days to the present, and provides coverage of Pope John Paul II's historic trip to Cuba in 1998.

▶**Cuba Reefs**
At this *National Geographic* Web site you can explore the reefs off Cuba. Here you can read articles about the reefs, view multimedia presentations, and view photographs of interesting underwater life.

▶**Cuba's Commercial Aviation History and the Pichs Collection**
At this Smithsonian Web site you will learn about the history of aviation in Cuba, including the beginnings of air mail to and from the island.

▶**Cuban Heritage Collection**
The University of Miami's Cuban Heritage Collection Web site offers online exhibits about Cuban exiles, revolutionary Cuba, and Cuban life and culture. It also contains an archive of digital images.

▶**FactMonster: Cuba**
From FactMonster.com, you can get information about Cuba. Learn about the economy, government, history, and culture of this island nation.

▶**Fact Monster: Ten Years' War**
Fact Monster.com provides a brief description of the Ten Years' War. The war was a bloody conflict for Cuban independence in which Cuban rebels fought the Spanish army from 1868 to 1878.

▶**1492: An Ongoing Voyage**
At this Library of Congress Web site you can explore the expeditions of Christopher Columbus. Here you will learn how Columbus landed in the Caribbean in 1492.

▶**Granma International**
At the Granma International Web site you can read news related to current events in Cuba.

Any comments? Contact us: comments@myreportlinks.com

## Report Links

**The Internet sites described below can be accessed at http://www.myreportlinks.com**

▶**José Martí: Apostle of Cuban Independence**
At this site you can read a biography of José Martí, known as the father of Cuban independence.

▶**The Legend of Hatuey**
This site covers the legend of Hatuey, a Taíno Indian chief who led a group of Cuban natives in a fight against the Spanish conquerors.

▶**PoliSci.com: Cuba**
PoliSci.com provides a profile of Cuba and information about Cuba's government. Included are examinations of Cuba's executive branch, legislative branch, judiciary, local governments, political parties, and more.

▶**Unfinished Business: Kennedy and Cuba**
At this Web site you will learn about major events involving Cuba that occurred during John F. Kennedy's administration, such as the Bay of Pigs invasion and the Cuban missile crisis.

▶**U.S. Department of State: Cuba**
The U.S. Department of State Web site provides information about Cuba including U.S.-Cuba relations, Cuba's history, human rights in Cuba, traveling in Cuba, and much more.

▶**U.S. Marines Land at Guantanamo Bay June 10, 1898**
America's Story from America's Library, a Library of Congress Web site, features the story of the first U.S. soldiers to land at Guantanamo Bay, Cuba, during the Spanish-American War. That war is known in Cuba as the Independence War.

▶**USS *Maine* Was Sunk February 15, 1898**
This feature from the Library of Congress tells the story of the USS *Maine*, whose explosion and sinking led to the Spanish-American War and eventually to Cuba's independence.

▶**The World of 1898: The Spanish-American War**
From this Library of Congress Web site you can read about the Spanish-American War, Cuba, and other countries involved in the conflict. Included are maps of Cuba.

Any comments? Contact us: **comments@myreportlinks.com**

## Cuba Facts

▶ **Official Name**
República de Cuba (Republic of Cuba)

▶ **Capital**
Havana

▶ **Population**
11,224,321[1]

▶ **Total Area**
42,803 square miles (110,860 square kilometers)

▶ **Highest Point**
Pico Turquino, 6,578 feet (2,005 meters)

▶ **Lowest Point**
Sea level along the coastline

▶ **Location**
The largest Caribbean island, Cuba lies 90 miles south of Florida.

▶ **Type of Government**
Communist state

▶ **Head of State**
President Fidel Castro (Ruz)

▶ **Monetary Unit**
Cuban peso

▶ **Official Language**
Spanish

▶ **National Anthem**
*La Bayamesa* ("The Bayamo Song"), which celebrates the Cuban rebels' victory over Spain in 1868, at the beginning of the Ten Years' War

▶ **National Flower**
Mariposa

▶ **National Tree**
Royal palm

▶ **National Bird**
Tocororo

▶ **National Flag**
The flag of Cuba, adopted in 1902, consists of five horizontal bands and a red triangle with a lone white star (*La Estrella Solitaria*). The three blue bands represent the three regions of Cuba at the time. The two white stripes represent the strength of Cuba's movement toward independence. The red triangle represents Cuban blood shed in its fight for independence from Spain. The single star originally represented an additional star for the Stars and Stripes, since some Cubans wanted the island to become part of the United States. The flag's design dates from 1849, to General Narciso Lopez, an Argentinian who attempted to liberate Cuba from Spanish rule.

**Chapter 1**

# Cuba: A Land of Beauty and Struggle

Cuba is a Caribbean island country. At first glance, Cuba seems like the ultimate tropical paradise. Shimmering waves lap at miles of unspoiled beaches. Warm sea breezes ruffle tall, elegant palms. People dance to music with an infectious Cuban beat.

But this paradise lies in the shadow of conflict. For five hundred years, Cubans have struggled to be free. The country was ruled first by Spain, then by the United States, then by a series of corrupt presidents and dictators. Fidel Castro seized power in 1959. Since then, Castro has ruled Cuba as a Communist state.

## ▶ The Father of Cuban Independence

Communist and anti-Communist Cubans agree on very little, but all Cubans admire José Martí, the most beloved figure in Cuban history.

José Martí was born in 1853 in Havana, the capital of Cuba. In 1869, sixteen-year-old Martí was arrested for supporting the Cuban independence movement. He was jailed and then deported to Spain. In 1881, Martí moved to New York where he worked as a journalist, wrote poetry and essays, and dedicated himself to freeing Cuba from Spain's rule. He organized exiled Cubans as volunteer revolutionary soldiers.

José Martí dreamed of an independent, democratic Cuba. He wanted to end racism and class distinctions, and he was able to unite Cuban exiles from all walks of life—rich, poor, white, black—in the independence cause.

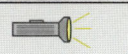

Cuba: A Land of Beauty and Struggle

▲ José Martí Square in Havana pays homage to the Cuban patriot and writer known as the father of Cuban independence.

Wealthy Cuban Americans contributed money, as did Cuban *tabaqueros* (cigar workers) in Florida, who gave 10 percent of their wages to Martí's independence movement.

In 1895, Martí sailed to Cuba to meet up with revolutionary forces. A month later they attacked the Spanish army. José Martí was one of the first Cubans killed in the battle.

Today, the airport in Havana is called José Martí International Airport. Streets and buildings in both Cuba and Cuban communities in the United States are named in honor of the revolutionary hero. Small statues of him appear in schools and public buildings. The Cuban government claims Martí as a symbol of the Communist revolution, and his birthday, January 28, is a national holiday.

Cuban Americans see Martí as a symbol of their struggle to free Cuba from communism. Cuban exiles in Miami broadcast anti-Communist radio and television programs that can be heard and seen in Cuba. Their broadcast stations are named Radio Martí and TV Martí.

## ▶ Americans in Cuba

In the first half of the twentieth century, Cuba was a popular vacation spot for wealthy Americans. During Prohibition, when the sale and manufacture of alcoholic beverages was banned in the United States, Americans could travel to Cuba and drink legally in bars and nightclubs.

Writer Ernest Hemingway visited Cuba during fishing trips he took from his home in Key West, Florida. In 1940, he moved to Cuba. Cubans loved Hemingway, whom they called *Ernesto*, and Hemingway loved Cuba. In 1954, when he won the Nobel Prize in Literature, he gave his medal to the Cuban people. Today his books are best-sellers in Cuba, and Cuban children study them in school. Hemingway's Cuban home, in a suburb of Havana, is a museum.

## ▶ Cubans in America

Throughout history, when Cubans wanted to flee political oppression or find better jobs, they often headed north to the United States. During the nineteenth century, thousands of Cubans fled to the United States during Cuba's battles for independence from Spain. Others traveled to the United States to work in Cuban-style cigar factories in Florida and New York. Cuba won independence in 1898, and during the first half of the twentieth century, Cubans continued to flee to the United States to escape poverty and the harsh regimes of Cuban dictators.

## ▶ Flights to Freedom

On January 1, 1959, Fidel Castro overthrew the Cuban government. Since then, more than a million Cubans have

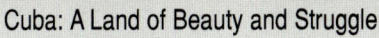

▲ *Gregorio Fuentes was Ernest Hemingway's boat captain while Hemingway lived in Cuba and is believed to have been the author's inspiration for the title character in* The Old Man and the Sea.

left their homeland to come to the United States. Between 1959 and 1962, Cuban immigrants streamed to Florida and New York. Some Cubans sent their children to the United States with help from the Catholic Church and charitable organizations. These children flew alone on what were called "Peter Pan" flights. It was often years before their parents could join them in the United States. In 1962 the American government stopped all commercial flights between the United States and Cuba, but Cubans continued to escape to the United States by first going through another country, such as Mexico or Spain.

In 1965, Castro announced that Cubans who had family in the United States could leave Cuba. Thousands of Cubans fled the country by boat. Afterward, the

American government again began allowing flights to Cuba. From 1965 to 1973, three hundred thousand Cubans immigrated to the United States on what became known as the "Freedom Flights." In 1973, the Cuban government halted these flights.

## ▶ The Marielitos

In 1980, a Cuban driver crashed his van into the Peruvian embassy in Havana and pleaded for asylum. Within hours, more than ten thousand Cubans had joined him. News agencies around the world reported on Cubans who crowded into the embassy, begging to leave the country.

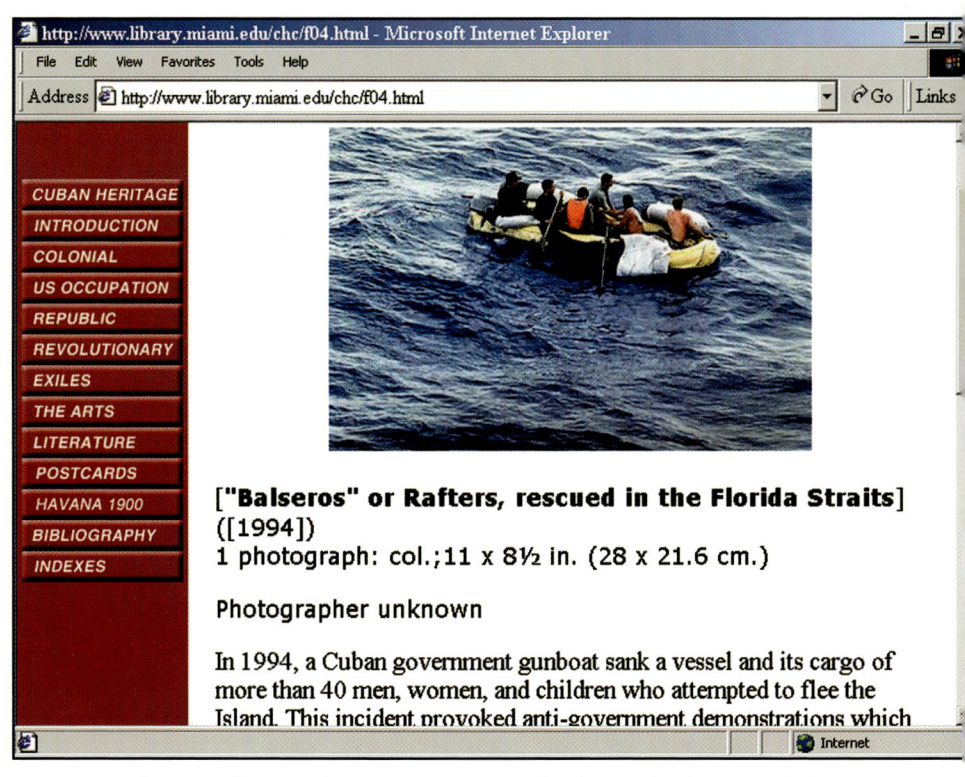

▲ This photograph captures a group of Cuban exiles known as balseros (for the balsas, or rafts, they use) being rescued in the Florida Straits in 1994.

Embarrassed, Castro announced that anyone who wanted to leave Cuba could depart from the port of Mariel. Cuban Americans sent boats from Florida to pick up the waiting Cubans. The operation became known as the Mariel Boatlift. The one hundred twenty-five thousand Cubans who fled were called *Marielitos*.

In the early 1990s, living conditions became so unbearable that thousands of Cubans tried to escape the island in rickety boats and rafts. The rafts, which Cubans call *balsas*, were often made of nothing more than inner tubes and fishing net. Many of the rafters, or *balseros*, drowned in their attempts to reach Florida.

## The Saga of Elián

At the end of the decade, the story of one little boy's attempt to flee Cuba by boat—and the custody battle that followed—captured the attention of Cubans and Americans. On Thanksgiving Day, 1999, two fishermen found five-year-old Elián González floating in an inner tube off the coast of Florida. Three days earlier, Elián, his mother, and ten other Cubans had boarded a homemade boat and sailed for the United States. The boat capsized, and nine of the balseros, including Elián's mother, drowned.

Elián's great-uncle, a Cuban exile living in Miami, took Elián in and insisted that he stay in the United States. The Cuban government demanded that he be returned to his father in Cuba. The American courts ruled that since Elián was a child, he should live with his closest living relative—his father. In June 2000, Elián's father took him back to Cuba.

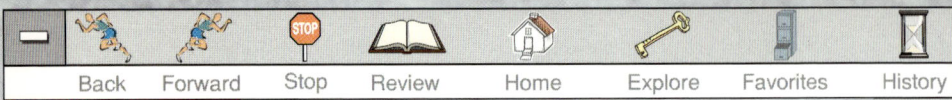

# Chapter 2

# Land and Climate

**C**uba is the largest Caribbean island. It is a long, thin sliver of land in the mouth of the Gulf of Mexico. Cuba lies 130 miles east of the Yucatán Peninsula of Mexico and only 90 miles south of Key West, Florida. In fact, Key West, Florida, is closer to Cuba than it is to Miami, Florida.

Cuba consists of the main island of Cuba, the smaller *Isla de la Juventud* ("Island of Youth"), and thousands of tiny islands and coral cays that ring the main island.

## ▶ The Lay of the Land

When Christopher Columbus first saw Cuba in 1492, he called the land "the most beautiful which eyes have seen,

▲ A map of Cuba.

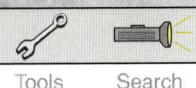

full of very good ports and deep rivers."[1] Cuba has a jagged coastline notched with bays that form deep, sheltered harbors. The capital city, Havana, is built on one of the safest harbors in the world, a large funnel-shaped bay with a long, narrow opening to the sea.

Plains and rolling farmland cover most of the island. On this flat land, Cuban farmers graze cattle and grow sugarcane, tobacco, rice, bananas, and citrus fruit.

Although Cuba is one of the least mountainous Caribbean islands, it does have three mountain ranges. The highest is the Sierra Maestra, which towers above the southern coast in eastern Cuba. These steep mountains push right up to the sea, where cliffs drop nearly straight down into the Caribbean. Pico Turquino, the highest point in Cuba, is in the Sierra Maestra. In 1956, when Fidel Castro and his rebel army began fighting against Cuba's government, they hid in the rugged Sierra Maestra.

The second-highest mountain range is the Sierra del Escambray along the southern coast of central Cuba. Dense forests cover these mountains, which get more rain per year than any other region in the country.

The lowest mountain range is the Cordillera de Guaniguanico at the western end of Cuba, in the province of Pinar del Río. The lush, green Viñales Valley lies within the Cordillera de Guaniguanico. In this valley, steep-sided hills rise up from the flatland like huge haystacks or loaves of bread. These rounded hills are called *mogotes*.

## ▶ Treasure Island

The country's second-largest island is the comma-shaped Isla de la Juventud, which lies south of the main island of Cuba.

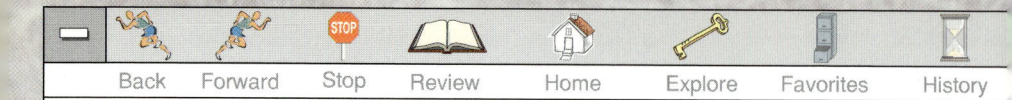

▲ *Pico Turquino, in Cuba's Sierra Maestra, is the country's highest peak, at 6,578 feet.*

While the Spanish were colonizing Cuba, they ignored the smaller Isla de la Juventud. It became a hideout for pirates, who called it Parrot Island after the many parrots that lived there. Later the island became a prison. José Martí and Fidel Castro both spent time there as political prisoners.

Pirates may not have left their gold behind, but Isla de la Juventud holds treasure of a different kind. In 1910, a French sailor was shipwrecked on the southeast coast of the island. He took shelter in caves nearby. There he found more than two hundred ancient pictographs, or cave paintings. The Ciboney, native people who lived in Cuba before the Spanish came, painted these pictures thousands of years ago. These pictographs are some of the most important cave paintings in the Caribbean.[2]

▶ **Two Seasons**

Cuba has a tropical climate. The temperature remains steady year-round, averaging between 70°F and 80°F.

Cuba has only two seasons: a wet season and a dry season. Trade winds known as *Vientos Alisios* generally blow year-round from the northeast.

The dry season lasts from December to April. The wet season lasts from May to November. Cuba receives more than 60 percent of its rainfall during the wet season. Cuba's rivers and streams are small, and many of them diminish to a trickle during the dry season, then swell to their banks during the wet season.

Cuba often finds itself in the path of hurricanes that rage across the Caribbean and the Gulf of Mexico. Although hurricanes can happen at any time of year, most hurricanes occur from June to November.

## ▶ The Environment

Cuba is a small country, but it has many different ecosystems. Rain forests cloak the mountains, especially on the windward side in the path of the moisture-laden trade winds. Cactus grows in dry areas of eastern Cuba, especially on the southern or leeward side of the prevailing winds. Tropical fish, sponges, and sea turtles live in the coral reefs that circle the island. Along the coast, crocodiles, water birds, and baby sharks flourish in mangrove swamps and wetlands.

Palm trees grow nearly everywhere on the island. Cuba has over thirty different kinds of palms. The slender, towering royal palm is Cuba's national tree.

Fragrant and colorful flowers cover the island. The *mariposa*, or butterfly jasmine, is the national flower. It is a delicate white flower that grows on riverbanks. The mariposa became a symbol of independence for Cubans during their fight for freedom from Spain.

More than three hundred species of birds can be found in Cuba, including flamingos, parrots, cuckoos, and the rare ivory-billed woodpecker. The *tocororo* is the national bird. Its brilliant red, white, and blue feathers are the same colors as the Cuban flag.

Cuba has some of the world's smallest animals. The bee hummingbird, which Cubans call the *zunzuncito*, is the smallest bird in the world. The male zunzuncito is one and a half inches (three and three-quarters centimeters) long, about the size of a grasshopper. It weighs about three-quarters ounce (two grams), which is less than the weight of a penny.

In 1996, scientists discovered a new species of frog in a mountain rain forest in eastern Cuba. The frog is black with an orange stripe, and it is only four-tenths inch (one centimeter) long. It is tied with a tiny Brazilian frog as the smallest frog in the world.[3]

When Columbus landed on Cuba, he found a land covered with forests. Over the next five centuries, most of the forests were cleared to make room for farms and sugar plantations. Trees were also cut for lumber and firewood. In the last few years, the Cuban government has begun replanting trees. The government also protects wildlife in national reserve areas, such as the Zapata Swamp. But Cuba is also beset by environmental problems: Havana Bay is one of the most polluted bodies of water in the Caribbean, and nickel mining has damaged the landscape and waters of the eastern end of Cuba near Moa Bay.[4]

## Chapter 3

# Culture

The Spanish began colonizing Cuba in the early 1500s. They soon brought slaves from Africa to work their plantations. Cuban slaves were usually kept together in their own tribal groups, so they were able to keep their customs alive. Over the years, Spanish and African traditions blended together to create Cuba's unique music, religion, and way of life.

Cubans today are a mix of races. Some Cubans are white descendants of Spanish settlers. Some Cubans are black descendants of slaves. Many Cubans are mulattoes, of mixed African and European ancestry. A few Cubans are part American Indian. In the nineteenth century, many Chinese came to Cuba as laborers, and some Cubans today are part Chinese. There is still a small "Chinatown" within Havana that includes a decorative entranceway into the Asian neighborhood.

## ▶ Rumba, Mambo, Cha-Cha-Cha!

In Cuba, music is everywhere. Cuban bands play in restaurants, cafés, and nightclubs. Cubans gather on street corners to play music and dance. In Cuba, music is simply a part of life.

Cuban music has been called "a love affair between the African drum and the Spanish guitar."[1] Spanish colonizers brought troubadour songs and flamenco music and dancing. Troubadours play guitars and sing romantic poems. Flamenco dancers clap their hands and click their heels and toes in rhythmic, complicated steps.

African slaves brought pulsing drumbeats. In Africa, drummers played to honor their kings. Drumming was also part of African religious ceremonies. African drummers played different drumbeats for different gods.

In Cuban cities, African and Spanish music combined to become the rhythmic and lively rumba. In the country, African and Spanish musical influences created the more melodious style of music known as the Cuban *son*. In the twentieth century, Cuban dances like the conga, mambo, and cha-cha-cha swept the world. In the 1980s, Cuban rhythms combined with pop music and jazz to become salsa.

Cuban musical instruments include the guitar, conga drum, bongos, claves, guiro, and maracas. Claves are

▲ The Basilica of the Virgin of Charity in El Cobre, west of Santiago, is visited by believers who leave behind offerings that include crutches, locks of hair, and even a piece of the Berlin Wall.

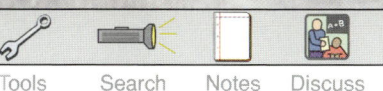

two hard wooden sticks that a musician clicks together. A guiro is a notched gourd played by scraping a stick along the notches.

## ▶ Religion

Many Cuban slaves were Yoruba people from western Africa. They believed in one supreme god surrounded by lesser gods called *orishas*.

The Spanish colonizers were Roman Catholic. They forced their African slaves to become Catholic, too. But the slaves secretly kept their own religion. The slaves saw similarities between their own orishas and Catholic saints and began worshiping the saints and orishas together. For example, they combined Santa Barbara, the saint who protects against lightning and storms, with Changó, the orisha of fire, thunder, and lightning. The African Yoruba religion blended with Catholicism to create *Santería*, which means "way of the saints."

When Fidel Castro took power, he banned religious holidays and expelled many Catholic priests from the country. In the new Communist state, only Communist party members could work in the best jobs, but Catholics could not join the Communist party. In order to survive, many Cubans stopped practicing religion.

During the 1990s, Castro began allowing more religious freedom. In 1996, he invited Pope John Paul II to visit Cuba. The pope accepted the invitation, and the Cuban government began preparing for his visit. In 1997, for the first time since Castro took power, Cubans were allowed to celebrate Christmas. In January 1998, the pope arrived in Cuba. It was the first time a pope had ever visited the island. The pope delivered mass in Havana as well as in several major cities, and millions of Cubans attended.

## The National Pastime

Cubans love baseball, which they call *beisbol*. Children in Cuba learn to play baseball when they are young. Cubans of all ages cheer for their favorite Cuban baseball teams.

Cubans first began playing baseball in the 1860s. At that time, Cubans were fighting for their independence from Spain. They loved baseball partly because it was not a Spanish game.

Baseball became even more popular in Cuba in the twentieth century. Team owners in the United States discovered that Cuban baseball players were very talented. Cuban players like Minnie Minoso, Bert Campaneris,

▲ The Cuban National League is made up of sixteen teams that play ninety games per season.

Tony Perez, and Luis Tiant moved to the United States to play on American teams.

After Castro came to power, it became harder for baseball players to leave Cuba. Many players risk their lives fleeing to the United States. Liván and Orlando Hernández are two such players. In 1995, when the Cuban national baseball team traveled to Mexico to play, Cuban pitcher Liván Hernández escaped from Cuban authorities and sneaked onto a flight to Venezuela. The next year he began pitching for the Florida Marlins. He was named Most Valuable Player in the 1997 World Series. He is now with the Montreal Expos.

After Liván left, Castro banned his brother, Orlando Hernández, from playing baseball in Cuba. In 1997, Orlando fled Cuba by boat. He signed a contract with the New York Yankees and pitched in the World Series in 1998, 1999, 2000, and 2001. In 2003, he was traded to the Chicago White Sox, who in turn traded him to the Montreal Expos, where he plays alongside his brother Liván.

Not all Cuban baseball players want to play for American teams, however. Although Cuban players earn very little money in Cuba, they are treated as celebrities in their homeland.

The Cuban government encourages athletics. Cuba has sports academies that train children who show athletic talent. The country has become a sports powerhouse, turning out world-class athletes in many sports. The Cuban national baseball team won the gold medal in the 1992 and 1996 Olympics. In the 2000 Olympics, Cuban athletes won gold in eleven sports, including boxing, wrestling, judo, tae kwon do, volleyball, and track and field.[2]

▲ *A young girl dressed for* la quinceañera *rides through the streets of Havana in a horse-drawn carriage.*

### ▶ The Big Birthday Party

When a Cuban girl reaches her fifteenth birthday, her family throws a lavish party called *la quinceañera*. Cuban families often start saving money for a daughter's quinceañera as soon as she is born.

The quinceañera, which resembles a wedding, is really a "coming-of-age" event for young women. The birthday girl dresses in a white gown similar to a wedding gown. Her friends wear matching gowns, as bridesmaids do. The boys wear suits and ties. Guests eat dinner and dance. They often arrive at the party in chauffeur-driven cars, which are mostly local taxis.

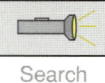

**Chapter 4** ▶

# Economy

The Spanish came to America looking for gold. In Cuba, they found no gold, but they did find tobacco and rich tropical land suited to growing sugarcane. Tobacco and sugar have been staples of the Cuban economy ever since.

▶ **Tobacco and Sugar**

When the Spanish arrived, the Taíno, an American Indian tribe, showed them tobacco. The Taíno smoked tobacco leaves wrapped in a big roll, which they called a *cohiba*. This was the first time the Spanish had seen a cigar. They

▲ *A tobacco field in Viñales. The tobacco used to make world-famous Cuban cigars is harvested and rolled by hand.*

took cigars back to Spain, where they became very popular. Europeans soon demanded the best cigars, and those cigars came from Cuba.

Tobacco grows best in areas with rich soil, high humidity, and plenty of sunshine, and the conditions in Cuba produce some of the highest-quality tobacco grown anywhere. Farmers tend their tobacco fields and dry their tobacco leaves with great care. Highly trained tabaqueros choose the best leaves. They hand roll the cigars in the same way that cigars have been rolled in Cuba for hundreds of years. Cuban cigars are still considered the finest in the world.

Cuba's tropical climate and fertile limestone soil are also perfect for growing sugarcane. The Spanish first planted sugarcane in Cuba in 1512. It soon became Cuba's most important crop. Before Castro took power, the United States bought most of Cuba's sugar. Many American companies owned Cuban sugarcane fields and sugar mills.

## ▶ After the Revolution

When Castro seized power, he also seized most private property. He nationalized sugar mills, businesses, and banks, putting them under the control of the government. Farmers who owned small farms were able to keep their land, but large farms and plantations were taken over by the government.

American companies owned much of this property. The Cuban government confiscated American-owned land and companies worth billions of dollars. In response, the American government stopped all trade between the United States and Cuba. The United States had been the main buyer of Cuban goods and had supplied Cuba with most of its imported goods. The American government believed the trade embargo would force Castro from power.

Castro instead turned to the Soviet Union for help. The former Soviet Union was a Communist state made up of fifteen republics. The largest of these republics was Russia. The Soviet Union began giving Cuba billions of dollars per year. The Soviet Union also bought most of Cuba's sugar and sent oil and machinery to Cuba.

Since the Cuban government owned all the businesses and most of the land, Cubans became government employees. Their wages were low, but the government guaranteed a job for every Cuban. The government also guaranteed free health care and education to its citizens. Still, living conditions were hard, and most Cubans were poor.

### ▶ The Special Period

In 1991, the Soviet Union broke apart. The fifteen Soviet republics declared themselves independent nations. These nations were no longer Communist, and they no longer sent money and supplies to Cuba. The Cuban economy collapsed.

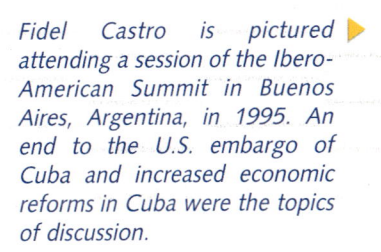

*Fidel Castro is pictured ▶ attending a session of the Ibero-American Summit in Buenos Aires, Argentina, in 1995. An end to the U.S. embargo of Cuba and increased economic reforms in Cuba were the topics of discussion.*

▲ *The rolling countryside of central Cuba features rich, fertile soil where fruits, vegetables, rice, and sugarcane are grown.*

Castro announced that Cubans were now entering the "Special Period in a Time of Peace." In the Special Period, every Cuban would have to make sacrifices. Food was rationed, and people waited in long lines to buy it. Each Cuban was allowed a meager supply of basic items, such as rice, sugar, beans, salt, coffee, and soap. Often, though, these items were not available in Cuban stores.

To save money, the government began turning off the electricity in different areas. These blackouts often lasted eighteen hours a day. Cubans had little money for gasoline for cars or buses. They began riding bicycles and using horse-drawn carts and bicycle taxis. Farmers who could not get fuel for their tractors began using oxen to work their fields and machetes to cut their crops by hand, as their forefathers had.

Factories, sugar mills, and other businesses closed. For the first time since the revolution, the Cuban government could not guarantee a job for every Cuban. To deal with unemployment, Castro began in 1993 to permit Cubans to own small family businesses, such as cafés or barbershops. The government also began in 1994 to allow farmers to sell some of their produce in farmers' markets.

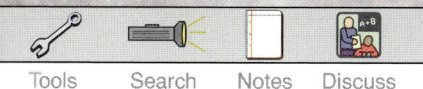

## The Return of the U.S. Dollar

For many years, American dollars had been illegal in Cuba. Cubans could be thrown in jail simply for having American money. In 1993, Castro decided to make the American dollar legal. Since then, Cuba has had two economies: one based on the Cuban peso and one based on the American dollar. Dollars are worth more than pesos, and some stores only accept American dollars. Bellboys, cabdrivers, and other workers who can earn dollars make more money than doctors and teachers who earn government wages paid in pesos. Cubans who have relatives in foreign countries, such as the United States, are also better off than other Cubans. Cuban Americans collectively send approximately $1 billion each year to their family members in Cuba. That money, known as remittance, is the largest source of income on the island of Cuba.

## An Improving Economy

Since the mid-1990s, the Cuban economy has started to improve. The government that once discouraged tourism now welcomes foreign visitors and the money those visitors spend. Cuba is building better hotels and restaurants to attract tourists.

Education is still free, and most Cubans can read and write. Cuba also has free child care and health care. Cuba's doctors are well trained, and Cubans have the highest life expectancy of any Latin American country.

## Chapter 5

# History

The first people to settle Cuba were the Ciboney. These American Indian people arrived on the island about 3500 B.C. The Ciboney lived in caves and fished and gathered fruit for sustenance.

Around A.D. 1100, another tribe began arriving on the island. They were the Taíno, and they came to Cuba to escape the fierce Carib warriors who were raiding other islands.

The Taíno lived in villages of round, palm-thatched huts. They made pottery and raised corn, yucca, and sweet potatoes. The Taíno were a peaceful people who welcomed Christopher Columbus to the island when he landed there in 1492. Columbus claimed the land that would become Cuba for Spain.

### ▶ Hatuey: Cuba's First Rebel

The island soon became known as Cuba, from the Taíno word *cubanacán*, meaning "central place." In 1512, Spanish colonizers began building towns in Cuba. They also began capturing American Indians to use as slaves.

According to legend, one Taíno chief, Hatuey, who had fled another island for Cuba, led a band of native people who fought back against the Spanish conquerors. Hatuey's strategy was to attack the Spaniards and then retreat into the hills, to regroup and plan future attacks. The Spanish military proved too strong, however, and Hatuey was captured and sentenced to burn at the stake.

A Spanish priest wanted to baptize Hatuey first, but the Taíno chief responded that he wanted nothing to do with a god whose people, the Spanish, had so brutalized his own.

The Spanish in Cuba continued to kill American Indians who resisted capture. They worked many more of them to death on plantations and in mines. The Spanish also brought diseases such as smallpox and measles to which the native people had no resistance, and many of them died. By the late 1500s, Spanish colonizers had wiped out nearly all the American Indians on the island.

The Spanish still needed workers for their plantations, however. With the Indians nearly gone, they began shipping slaves from Africa to Cuba.

### ▶ Fighting for Independence

Cuba's sugar, coffee, and tobacco plantations prospered, and Spain made a hefty profit from its colony. But by the mid-1800s, Cubans were tired of being ruled by Spain. Spain imposed unfair taxes and laws. The Spanish-born

▲ El Morro lighthouse overlooking Havana's harbor was built in 1845 on the grounds of the sixteenth-century Spanish fortress known as the Castillo de los Tres Reyes del Morro, or the El Morro Castle.

officials who governed Cuba dealt brutally with anyone who protested.

## American Attempts at Annexation

In 1844 a slave revolt in Cuba made Southern slaveholders in the United States fearful that Spain would abolish slavery on the island. Some Southern politicians were joined by Cuban slaveholders in trying to get the United States to annex Cuba. Other American political and military interests led the United States to offer to buy Cuba from Spain several times without success. With the beginning of the American Civil War, in 1861, America's interest in Cuba was put on hold. The United States' war with Spain near the end of the century would eventually result in Cuba's independence. Before that, however, many Cuban patriots gave their lives in their struggle to free themselves from Spanish rule.

## The Ten Years' War

In 1868, a landowner named Carlos Manuel de Céspedes freed his slaves. He and his followers declared Cuba an independent nation and began taking over eastern Cuba. Spain sent soldiers to put down these rebels. For the next decade, the Spanish army and Cuban rebels fought each other in a bloody conflict known as the Ten Years' War. By 1878, more than two hundred thousand people had died. The war had destroyed the Cuban economy, and American companies began buying plantations and sugar mills on the island. In 1886, Spain finally abolished slavery.

## José Martí: Father of Cuban Independence

José Martí was a writer, poet, and Cuban patriot who was jailed at the age of sixteen and exiled from his homeland during the Ten Years' War. In 1881 he moved to New York

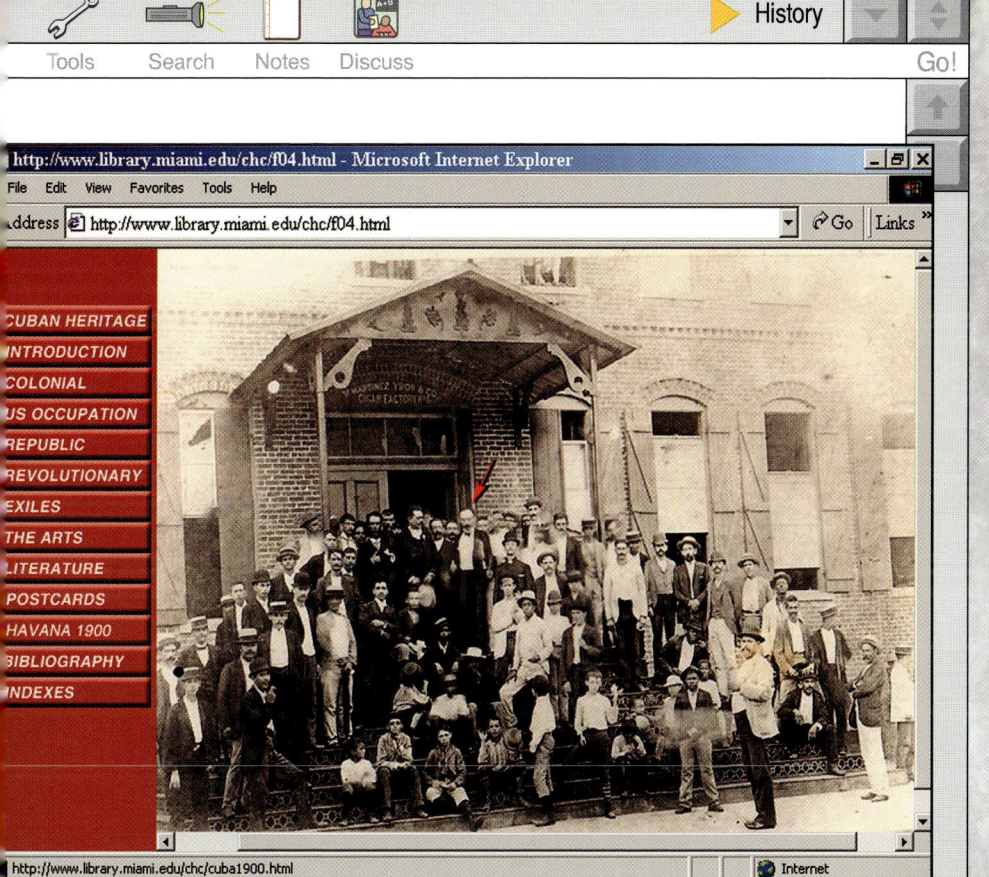

▲ As the exiled leader of the Cuban Revolutionary Party (CRP), José Martí worked for a time in the United States to free Cuba from Spanish rule. Here he is with delegates of the CRP on the steps of a tobacco factory in Tampa, Florida.

City and spent the next fourteen years rallying support for Cuban independence. It was in New York that he founded the Cuban Revolutionary Party. In 1895, he secretly sailed back to Cuba. He met up with rebel forces led by Máximo Goméz and Antonio Macéo, two generals who had fought against Spain in the Ten Years' War. On May 19, 1895, the Cuban rebels attacked the Spanish in the battle of Dos Ríos. José Martí charged into battle and was one of the first to be killed.

35

## The Independence War

Fierce fighting continued for the next three years, and the Cubans succeeded in driving the Spanish from eastern Cuba. In 1898, the United States sent the battleship *Maine* to Cuba to protect Americans and American property. The *Maine* exploded and sank in Havana Harbor, killing 260 American sailors. Nobody ever discovered why the *Maine* exploded, but at the time, Americans blamed Spain, and the United States declared war on that nation. Four months later, Spain was defeated in what is known as the Spanish-American War. In Cuba, this war is called the Independence War.

## Free at Last . . . Sort Of

The Independence War freed Cuba from Spain, but Cubans still did not have self-rule. The United States military occupied Cuba for the next three and a half years. In 1902, Cuba officially became an independent republic, but the United States forced Cuba to include the Platt Amendment in the new Cuban constitution. This amendment allowed the United States to obtain land in Cuba for naval bases and to protect American property in Cuba through the use of military force.

Cubans resented the Platt Amendment for the power it gave the United States. Cubans could now elect their own government, but they knew the United States had a great deal of influence over that government. American troops returned to Cuba in 1906 when opposition to the Cuban government led to a rebellion. From 1906 to 1909, Cuba was governed by a civil-military government led by an American administrator, Charles Magoon. A second Cuban republic was established in 1909, but

▲ *The explosion and sinking of the USS* Maine *in Havana Harbor on February 15, 1898, led the United States to declare war on Spain, resulting in the Spanish-American War. In Cuba, the conflict is known as the Independence War.*

uprisings in 1912 and 1917 led to further American military intervention to protect the American companies in Cuba.

### ▶ Dictators and Destruction

For the remaining first half of the twentieth century, Cuba was ruled by a string of corrupt presidents. These presidents made themselves rich while most Cubans became poorer and poorer. Gerardo Machado, president from 1925 to 1933, was a brutal dictator. He ignored the constitution and jailed, tortured, and killed his enemies.

Fulgenció Batista controlled Cuba from 1934 to 1944 and seized power again in 1952. At first, Batista seemed to be a strong leader, concerned with improving the living conditions in his country. In 1934, the United States agreed to repeal the Platt Amendment although it continued to lease a naval base at Guantánamo Bay. But Batista turned out to be a corrupt and cruel dictator. He, too, tortured and killed his enemies. He allowed American gangsters to take over Cuban nightclubs and casinos.

## The Arrival of Fidel Castro

One of Batista's political enemies was a young lawyer named Fidel Castro. Castro tried to overthrow Batista's government on July 26, 1953, when he attacked an army garrison in Santiago de Cuba, but he was captured and imprisoned. Once free, Castro began training a rebel army in Mexico. He named the army the Twenty-sixth of July Movement, after the date of his attack. In 1957, Castro and eighty-one followers sailed back to Cuba. They made their way into the Sierra Maestra and set up their guerrilla base.

Thousands of Cubans joined the rebellion. Castro's rebel army took over towns and launched attacks on Batista's Cuban army. Batista realized that the rebels would soon control all of Cuba. On December 31, 1958, he fled the country with the help of the United States. One week later, Castro rolled into Havana atop a tank to declare victory. He became the premier of Cuba and later would be called president of the Council of State and Council of Ministers, Cuba's Communist regime. Castro was at first hailed as a liberator by many Cubans, and he did make reforms to help the country's poor people. But he was soon found to be ruthless.

Castro began rounding up Cubans he believed had supported Batista. Many of these people were shot by firing squad. Castro gradually seized private property and

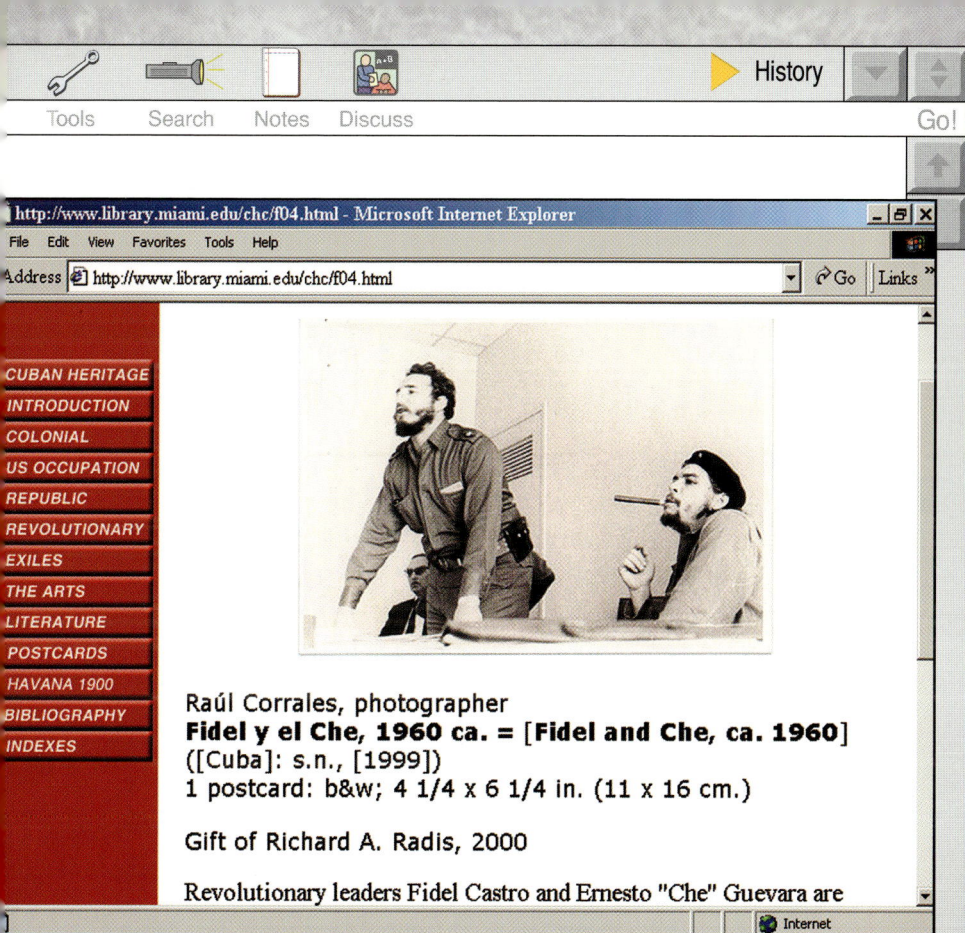

▲ Young revolutionaries Fidel Castro (left) and Che Guevara (right) are pictured in 1960. Guevara, from Argentina, helped steer Cuba toward the Soviet Union and away from the United States.

took away the freedom of the press. Once the United States stopped trading with Cuba, Castro signed trade agreements with the Soviet Union, the largest and most powerful Communist country at the time.

### ▶ The Bay of Pigs Invasion

Many Cubans, terrified by Castro's actions, left the country. With the encouragement and financial support of the United States government, about fifteen hundred of these exiles formed a counterrevolutionary army to overthrow Castro. On April 17, 1961, this exile army landed at the Bay of Pigs

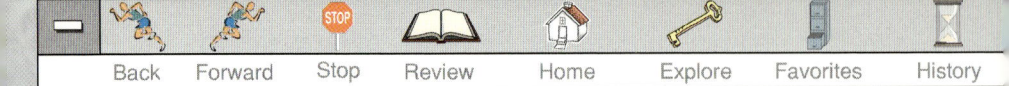

(*Bahia de Cochinos*) in southern Cuba. They had been promised help from the United States military, but that help never came. Within three days, Castro's army had defeated the exiles and taken most of them prisoner. In December 1962, Castro released the exiles in exchange for $53 million in food and medical supplies from the United States.

### ▶ The Cuban Missile Crisis

In 1962, the United States discovered that the Soviet Union was building a nuclear missile base in Cuba. The president of the United States, John F. Kennedy, sent American warships to block Cuban ports. He demanded that the Soviet Union remove the missiles. If not, the United States would invade Cuba. For several days in October 1962, the world waited, wondering if the two most powerful nations in the world—the United States and the Soviet Union—would become involved in a nuclear war. Finally, the Soviet Union backed down and agreed to remove the missiles.

Fidel Castro is still Cuba's president. He has ruled for over forty years, longer than any other current world leader. In 1991, the Soviet Union collapsed, leaving Cuba one of the few remaining Communist countries.

# Chapter 6

# Cuban Americans

Throughout modern history, Cubans seeking safety or a better life have come to the United States. But the trickle of Cuban immigrants became a flood when Fidel Castro took power. Since 1959, over a million Cubans have fled to the United States. The majority—over five hundred thousand—have settled in Miami. Union City, New Jersey, has the second-highest population of Cuban Americans.

## Exiles or Immigrants?

The first groups to flee Castro's government were business people and professionals. They were middle class or wealthy in Cuba, but when they came to the United States, they had to leave their money and property behind. In fact, after 1961, Cubans leaving the country could not take more than $5 with them.

When they reached the United States, many Cubans found that they could not work in the professions they had trained for. Doctors and lawyers could not practice medicine or law because their Cuban licenses were not valid in the United States. Highly educated Cubans had to take jobs as cabdrivers or waitresses.

Still, these new Cuban Americans were determined to be successful. They settled together in large Cuban-American communities, such as Little Havana in Miami. Since they could not find jobs that paid well, they created their own. Cuban Americans opened cafés and shops, and later banks, car dealerships, and other large businesses.

Cuban Americans have become one of the most financially successful immigrant groups in the United States.

Cuban Americans who fled Cuba in the 1960s tend to think of themselves as exiles rather than immigrants. When they came to the United States, they did not think they would stay long. They believed that they would return to Cuba once Castro was defeated. Over the years, they have realized they are in the United States to stay. Still, they toast each other with the words "Next year in Havana!" They also do their best to keep their Cuban traditions and culture alive.

Cubans who fled during the Mariel Boatlift in 1980 or as balseros in the 1990s know they are immigrants. Most of these Cuban Americans were not wealthy in Cuba. They came to the United States seeking a better life for themselves and their families.

## Politics

Cuban Americans are politically active. They vote in high numbers and lobby for causes they believe in. The cause that almost all Cuban Americans agree on is that Cuba must be freed from Castro's harsh government.

Florida has two Cuban-American representatives in the United States Congress. Representative Ileana Ros-Lehtinen was born in Havana. She and her family fled to the United States when she was seven years old. She became the first Cuban-born woman to serve in the Florida house of representatives and the Florida senate. In 1989 she was elected to the United States House of Representatives, becoming the first Hispanic woman to serve in Congress.

Lincoln Diaz-Balart also served in the Florida house and Florida senate. He was elected to the U.S. House of Representatives in 1992. Representative Diaz-Balart is the

**[Domino Park, Little Havana, Miami]**
([1994])
1 photograph: col.; 4 x 6 in. (10.1 x 15.1 cm.)

Photographer unknown

The City of Miami Máximo Gómez Park, known as Domino Park, is a popular gathering place in Miami's Little Havana where domino aficionados pass the hours discussing politics over a friendly game. As

▲ Little Havana is an area of Miami, Florida, that has become home to many Cuban exiles. Here, Cuban-Americans play dominoes in Máximo Gómez Park.

nephew of Mirta Diaz-Balart, Castro's first wife. He is the first cousin of Castro's son, Fidelito.

New Jersey Representative Robert Menendez is a second-generation Cuban American. He began his political career as the mayor of Union City, New Jersey. He went on to become a New Jersey state assemblyman and state senator. He was elected to the United States House of Representatives in 1992.

## ▶ Famous Cuban Americans

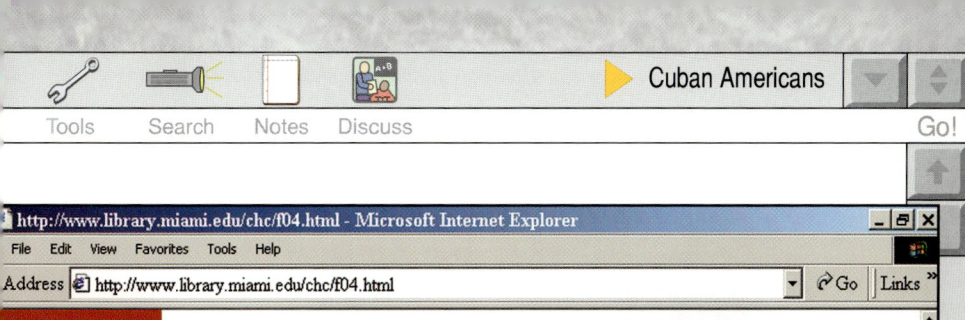

Cuban music swept through the United States in the 1940s and has remained popular ever since. Many of the

*Congresswoman Ileana Ros-Lehtinen represents Florida's eighteenth congressional district. Born in Havana, she and her family left Cuba in 1959 following Castro's rise to power. She was the first Hispanic woman elected to the United States Congress.*

most famous Cuban Americans are musicians.

Desi Arnaz is perhaps the most famous. Arnaz was born in Santiago, Cuba, in 1917. He and his mother fled the country in 1933, after the fall of the Machado government. In the United States, Arnaz became a successful bandleader, acted in twenty movies, and also appeared on Broadway. In 1951, he and his wife, Lucille Ball, created and starred in *I Love Lucy*, the most popular television series in history. Fifty years later, reruns of the show still play in countries around the world.[1]

More recently, Cuban-American singer Gloria Estefan and her band, the Miami Sound Machine, have mixed traditional Cuban rhythms with American pop music. Estefan was born in Havana in 1957. When Castro came to power, she and her family fled the country. Her father returned to Cuba in the Bay of Pigs invasion. He was captured and spent almost two years in a Cuban prison. In 1985, the Miami Sound Machine won the American Music Award as best new pop artist.

Other Cuban-American musicians include Grammy-winning singer Celia Cruz, known as "The Queen of Salsa," and world-renowned jazz trumpeter Arturo Sandoval, who defected from Cuba in 1990. When Cruz passed away on July 16, 2003, Latin music lovers the world over mourned her death, and Cubans as well as Cuban Americans paid her tribute. In her native land, however, the Communist party newspaper in Havana dedicated only two paragraphs to her obituary, since she was an exile who had criticized the Castro regime.

Cuban music has inspired the writing of Cuban-American novelist Oscar Hijuelos. Hijuelos won the 1990 Pulitzer Prize for Fiction for his novel *The Mambo Kings Play Songs of Love.* This book tells the story of two Cuban brothers, both musicians, who move to New York in the 1940s. The book was made into the movie *The Mambo Kings* starring Antonio Banderas.

Cuban-American WNBA star Rebecca Lobo led the University of Connecticut Lady Huskies to a national championship in 1995. She won an Olympic gold medal as a member of the U.S. women's basketball team in 1996.

Cuban Americans are proud of their Cuban heritage. They are also grateful to live in the United States where they are free to pursue their dreams. Cuban Americans have taken advantage of this freedom and have excelled in many professions, from politics and business to sports, science, and the arts.

## Chapter Notes

### Cuba Facts

1. "Cuba," *The World Factbook 2002*, January 1, 2002, <http://www.cia.gov/cia/publications/factbook/geos/cu.html> (November 23, 2002).

### Chapter 2. Land and Climate

1. Edward Everett Hale, *The life of Christopher Columbus,* n.d., <http://www.classicreader.com/read.php/sid.2/bookid.1293/sec.5> (November 24, 2002).

2. Ramón Dacal Moure and Manuel Rivero de la Calle, translated by Daniel H. Sandweiss, *Art and Archaeology of Pre-Columbian Cuba,* Daniel H. Sandweiss and David R. Watters, eds. (Pittsburgh: University of Pittsburgh Press, 1996), p. 30.

3. Barbara K. Kennedy, "Scientists Discover Smallest Frog," November 22, 1996, <http://www.science.psu.edu/alert/FROG.htm> (November 24, 2002).

4. Sergio Diaz-Briquets and Jorge Pérez-López, *Conquering Nature: The Environmental Legacy of Socialism in Cuba* (Pittsburgh: University of Pittsburgh Press, 2000), pp. 245–247.

### Chapter 3. Culture

1. *Roots of Rhythm*, videotape (New York: New Video Group, 1994).

2. "Olympic Medal Winners," *International Olympic Committee*, 2002, n.d. <http://www.olympic.org/uk/athletes/results/search_r_uk.asp> (November 24, 2002).

### Chapter 6. Cuban Americans

1. Michael McClay, *I Love Lucy* (New York: Warner Books, 1995), p. xi.

## Further Reading

Chrisp, Peter. *The Cuban Missile Crisis.* Milwaukee: World Almanac Library, 2002.

Fox, Mary Virginia. *Cuba.* San Diego: Lucent Books, 1999.

Gonzales-Pando, Miguel. *The Cuban Americans.* Westport, Conn.: Greenwood Press, 1998.

Hahn, Laura D. *The Cuban Americans.* Farmington Hills, Mich.: Mason Crest Publishers, 2002.

Hoobler, Dorothy, and Thomas Hoobler. *The Cuban American Family Album.* New York: Oxford University Press, 1996.

Jacobs, Francine. *The Tainos.* New York: G. P. Putnam's Sons, 1992.

Luis, William. *Culture and Customs of Cuba.* Westport, Conn.: Greenwood Press, 2001.

Mendez, Adriana. *Cubans in America.* Minneapolis: Lerner Publishing Group, 1994.

Morrison, Marion. *Cuba.* Austin, Tex.: Raintree Steck-Vaughn, 1998.

Olsen, James S., and Judith E. Olsen. *The Cuban Americans: From Trauma to Triumph.* Farmington Hills, Mich.: Gale Group, 1995.

Perez, Louis A. *On Becoming Cuban: Identity, Nationality, and Culture.* New York: The Ecco Press, 2001.

Smith, Wayne S. *Portrait of Cuba.* Atlanta: Turner Publishing, Inc., 1991.

Thomas, Hugh. *Cuba: The Pursuit of Freedom.* New York: Macmillan Publishing, 2001.

# Index

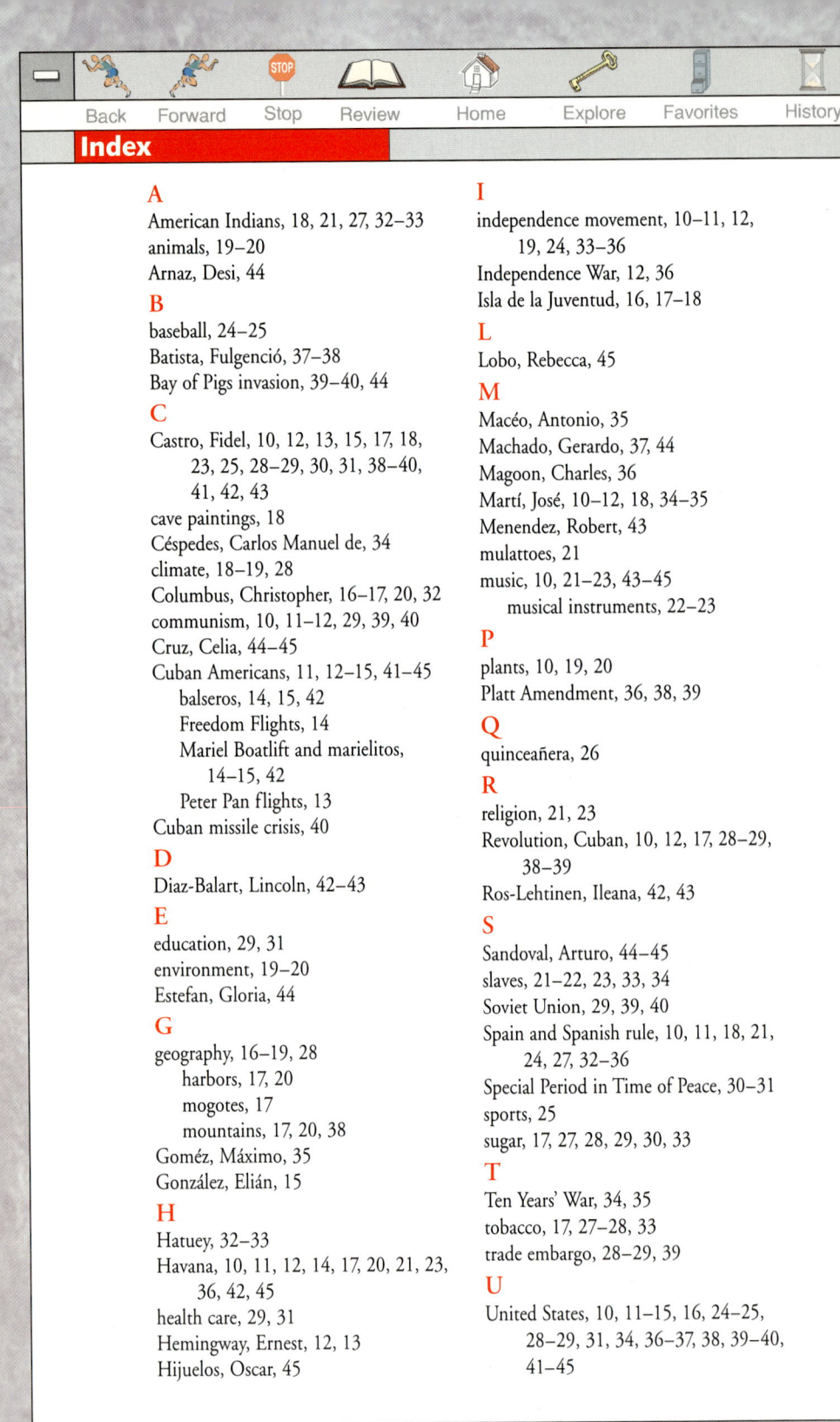

## A
American Indians, 18, 21, 27, 32–33
animals, 19–20
Arnaz, Desi, 44

## B
baseball, 24–25
Batista, Fulgencio, 37–38
Bay of Pigs invasion, 39–40, 44

## C
Castro, Fidel, 10, 12, 13, 15, 17, 18, 23, 25, 28–29, 30, 31, 38–40, 41, 42, 43
cave paintings, 18
Céspedes, Carlos Manuel de, 34
climate, 18–19, 28
Columbus, Christopher, 16–17, 20, 32
communism, 10, 11–12, 29, 39, 40
Cruz, Celia, 44–45
Cuban Americans, 11, 12–15, 41–45
　　balseros, 14, 15, 42
　　Freedom Flights, 14
　　Mariel Boatlift and marielitos, 14–15, 42
　　Peter Pan flights, 13
Cuban missile crisis, 40

## D
Diaz-Balart, Lincoln, 42–43

## E
education, 29, 31
environment, 19–20
Estefan, Gloria, 44

## G
geography, 16–19, 28
　　harbors, 17, 20
　　mogotes, 17
　　mountains, 17, 20, 38
Goméz, Máximo, 35
González, Elián, 15

## H
Hatuey, 32–33
Havana, 10, 11, 12, 14, 17, 20, 21, 23, 36, 42, 45
health care, 29, 31
Hemingway, Ernest, 12, 13
Hijuelos, Oscar, 45

## I
independence movement, 10–11, 12, 19, 24, 33–36
Independence War, 12, 36
Isla de la Juventud, 16, 17–18

## L
Lobo, Rebecca, 45

## M
Macéo, Antonio, 35
Machado, Gerardo, 37, 44
Magoon, Charles, 36
Martí, José, 10–12, 18, 34–35
Menendez, Robert, 43
mulattoes, 21
music, 10, 21–23, 43–45
　　musical instruments, 22–23

## P
plants, 10, 19, 20
Platt Amendment, 36, 38, 39

## Q
quinceañera, 26

## R
religion, 21, 23
Revolution, Cuban, 10, 12, 17, 28–29, 38–39
Ros-Lehtinen, Ileana, 42, 43

## S
Sandoval, Arturo, 44–45
slaves, 21–22, 23, 33, 34
Soviet Union, 29, 39, 40
Spain and Spanish rule, 10, 11, 18, 21, 24, 27, 32–36
Special Period in Time of Peace, 30–31
sports, 25
sugar, 17, 27, 28, 29, 30, 33

## T
Ten Years' War, 34, 35
tobacco, 17, 27–28, 33
trade embargo, 28–29, 39

## U
United States, 10, 11–15, 16, 24–25, 28–29, 31, 34, 36–37, 38, 39–40, 41–45